Original title:
Timber Tunes

Copyright © 2025 Creative Arts Management OÜ
All rights reserved.

Author: Vivian Laurent
ISBN HARDBACK: 978-1-80567-337-8
ISBN PAPERBACK: 978-1-80567-636-2

Serenade of the Sylvan

In a forest full of chatter,
Squirrels dance with glee,
A raccoon plays the fiddle,
While birds croon in harmony.

The trees sway with their giggles,
As branches tap their feet,
A bear joins in the waltz,
With steps surprisingly neat.

Frogs leap in a chorus,
While crickets strum a tune,
The loons laugh in the distance,
Beneath the smiling moon.

Amidst all this commotion,
The owls hoot with a grin,
Nature's grand performance,
Let the laughter begin!

Melodies in the Maple

In the shade of leafy branches,
A chipmunk starts to sing,
His acorn cap a stage hat,
Oh, what joy the woods bring!

The wind plays soft maracas,
Tickling every leaf,
While the bumblebees buzz happily,
Creating quite a mischief.

A shy old turtle claps along,
With rhythm oh so slow,
But his shell hits like a drum,
Steady as the show!

With laughter in the twilight,
The trees begin to sway,
Nature's silly serenade,
It brightens up the day!

Ballad of the Birch

Underneath the silver birch,
A fox dons a pairs of shades,
He struts along the forest path,
In wacky woodland parades.

Frolicking with the foliage,
A squirrel steals the scene,
He does a little jig, you see,
To keep his acorns clean.

The porcupine rolls his eyes,
At antics so absurd,
While giggling in the background,
Are chattering woodpeckers.

With branches swaying side to side,
And laughter filled with cheer,
The woodland's wacky ballad plays,
No worries, only beer!

Rustling Rhythms

Among the leaves, the rustling,
A dance that swings with style,
While ants march to a drumbeat,
In marching line, they file.

A caterpillar flips and flops,
With moves that raise a grin,
While butterflies flutter by,
And twirl with balletic spin.

Rabbits hop to playful beats,
With giggles all around,
And snails slide in a groove so smooth,
They'll give you quite a clown.

The breeze whispers soft secrets,
And nature joins the fun,
As leaves applaud the rhythm,
Under the warming sun!

Lament of the Willow

The willow weeps with a giggly sway,
It tells the breeze to come out and play.
With branches long and a twisty dance,
It chuckles loud at every chance.

Its leaves titter in a whispering gale,
Swishing and swaying like a comical tale.
The nearby oak gives a dignified nod,
But the willow just laughs, quite unflawed.

A squirrel scampers, a partner in jest,
Climbs the long arms of its leafy crest.
Together they frolic, a silly parade,
In a whimsical world where joy's displayed.

Oh gentle willow, how you inspire,
With your laughter that never seems to tire.
Through every twist and every bend,
Your humor is something we all commend.

Rustic Reverberations

In the forest where the wild things giggle,
A chorus of chirps makes the trees wiggle.
Branches creak in a merry tune,
While the sun shines down like a playful boon.

A bunny hops, wearing a grin so wide,
It leaps on logs, with no reason to hide.
The chirping birds join in the jest,
Singing songs that put joy to the test.

Woodpeckers tap to a funky beat,
While the leaves dance under tiny feet.
A deer prances, with a skip and a bound,
In the laughter of nature, pure joy is found.

Oh rustic scene, so filled with cheer,
Echoes of laughter ring loud and clear.
With every rustle, a funny surprise,
In this woodland haven, where humor flies.

The Hidden Harmony

Underneath the tall oak's shade,
A secret song is playfully made.
Rustling leaves in a breezy hum,
Make the forest feel so glum.

A critter chuckles from behind the bark,
Sharing jokes that get quite a spark.
The mushrooms giggle with spots so bold,
While the trees whisper tales of old.

A chipmunk joins in with a cheeky grin,
Dancing like it knows it can't win.
The forest floor shudders with mirth,
As laughter echoes throughout the earth.

In this hidden nook of gleeful delight,
Nature's harmony shines ever bright.
With silly sounds and joyful play,
In every critter, a dancer at bay.

Echoing Elms

In the shade of elms so grand and wise,
A chorus of laughter fills the skies.
With every rustle of a leafy heart,
The echoes of fun begin to start.

Two squirrels chase, with tails like ribbons,
Dodging branches, their laughter given.
The breeze joins in, with a playful shove,
As the elms watch, with a smile of love.

A jester crow swoops down from afar,
Telling puns beneath the bright star.
With wings flapping to the rhythm so light,
The elms sway along, what a sight!

So here in this grove, the funny prevails,
With stories and jokes painted in trails.
In the heart of nature, joy never fails,
As echoing elms dance with breezy tales.

Harmonious Hues of the Hearth

Bouncing beams with smiles so bright,
Chasing shadows, what a sight!
Logs that crackle, giggles play,
In the warmth, we joke away.

Dancing fires flicker and sway,
Whimsical whispers lead the way.
S'mores are flying, oh what fun,
Catching treats under the sun!

Bark and laughter, cozy space,
Nature's tunes fill up the place.
Wooden benches filled with cheer,
Friends around, we all draw near.

In the glow, the night is bright,
As stories soar to newfound heights.
With each laugh, the shadows twirl,
A symphony of joy unfurl.

The Gathered Greenery's Anthem

Leaves are chattering with delight,
In the sun, everything feels right.
Branches shake in playful jest,
Nature's band, we are the best!

Mossy cushions, soft and sweet,
As we stomp our dancing feet.
Bugs join in, they take the stage,
Uninvited, but so engaged!

Vines are twirling round the oaks,
Mischief brews as laughter pokes.
Join the tune, don't miss a beat,
Adventure waits with every greet!

Gathered friends, with glee we sing,
Celebrating every little thing.
Nature's chorus, loud and free,
In this green space, joy's the key.

Pitches from the Pinecones

Pinecones tumble, roll away,
Bouncing off, oh what a play!
Squirrels join the crazy race,
Chasing echoes, finding space!

Saplings sway with giddy glee,
Climbing up for all to see.
Laughter lingers in each ring,
Nature's cheer, in spring we sing!

Needles dance on gentle breeze,
Rustling tunes put minds at ease.
Is it laughter, is it bark?
Every note ignites a spark!

Gather 'round, all friends and foes,
Piney songs, where giggling grows.
Ringing bells with nature's voice,
In this harmony, we rejoice.

Melodic Murmurs at Dusk

As the sun dips, crickets tune,
To a melody of the moon.
Branches giggle, twigs applaud,
Every sound seems like a fraud!

Fireflies wink with little lights,
Whispering secrets through the nights.
Hooting owls, watch the show,
In this playful, wobbly flow!

Breezes bring a silly tune,
Rustling leaves, like a cartoon.
With a chuckle, shadows blend,
Nature's laughter without end.

Gather here, let joy cascade,
In the twilight, fun is made.
With each sparkle, every hum,
Nighttime's song, we all succumb.

Forest Harmonies

In the woods, a squirrel ballet,
Twists and twirls, a nutty display.
Branches tap dance with a light,
As birds join in, taking flight.

A raccoon plays a drum of pine,
While rabbits hop, all in line.
Frogs croak their bass, out of tune,
Amidst the trees, they have a swoon.

The fox brings a flute, quite the show,
Whistling tunes that make leaves flow.
Jays drop low, creating a choir,
With laughter rising, lifting higher.

So come to the woods, join the fun,
Where every critter knows how to run.
In this concert, we're all part,
An orchestra made straight from the heart.

Whispers of the Woods

A bear with a horn plays a shy tune,
While skunks strut their stuff beneath the moon.
A beaver taps on a hollowed log,
As owls join in, keeping the fog.

Hooting and tooting, the night is bright,
Squirrels chatter with all of their might.
The trees sway, they sway to the beat,
While the groundhog taps his little feet.

Echoes bounce off of mossy stones,
As critters dance in their merry zones.
Chirping crickets lend their sound,
In this wild party, joy is found.

So come take a stroll, hear the sounds,
In the woods, laughter and music abounds.
Amongst the ferns and cool, crisp air,
Join the woodland fun, if you dare!

Serenade of the Saplings

Little saplings sway in the breeze,
Singing soft songs, they aim to please.
A bumbling bee buzzes the tune,
As tadpoles join with a splashy croon.

A tiny worm plays a string of grass,
While beetles march, letting time pass.
Sunlight glimmers, lighting the show,
As flowers dance with a colorful flow.

With each note, a giggle follows,
As frogs make plops in their leafy hollows.
The elder trees rock their wise old sway,
In playful harmony, come what may.

So let's gather 'round, join the spree,
In nature's concert, wild and free.
With every flutter, every cheer,
The serenade calls for all to hear!

Echoes Beneath the Canopy

Beneath the green, there's quite a show,
With critters joining, the fun will flow.
A chipmunk strums on a twiggy guitar,
While a wise owl sways, near and far.

Rascally raccoons bring their own snacks,
As the hedgehog sings, it's all about tracks.
Bouncing branches beat the drum,
To this silly rhythm, we all come.

Acorns drop with a friendly plop,
As the woodpecker doesn't want to stop.
Hilarity echoes, a woodland spree,
A melody woven with glee and glee.

So tiptoe along, let giggles reign,
In this woodland orchestra, joy is the gain.
With every rustle and joyous cheer,
Let's dance to the laughter, bring your good cheer!

The Nature's Nocturne

Under the moon, a squirrel pranced,
Dancing leaves, as if enhanced.
The crickets chirp, a comical rhyme,
While owls groan, in nighttime's prime.

A raccoon wears a mask with flair,
Stealing snacks while folks do stare.
The breeze whispers jokes, but none can hear,
Just trees chuckle, year after year.

Bats flit by, with style and grace,
In this woodland, a lively place.
They swoop and dive, as if in a race,
Nature's own merry, silly space.

The night concludes with a loud croak,
A frog's joke, all wild and broke.
Laughter echoes in the wood so clear,
Nature's night song, a joy to hear.

Forest Folk Melodies

Frogs in tuxedos, singing on logs,
Underneath the moon like overgrown frogs.
The owls join in, their wisdom so bright,
But who knows if they sing right?

Squirrels tap dance on the old oak tree,
While chipmunks chime in with glee.
Their little feet beat a merry drum,
As the forest echoes, 'Here comes fun!'

The sun peeks out, the show goes on,
While a bear yawned, stretching with brawn.
He juggled berries with a humorous flair,
And all of us laughed 'cause he didn't care.

A tune for the critters, a whirl to behold,
Each note a story, silly and bold.
From shy little mice with a wink in their eyes,
To the trees swaying, touching the skies.

Rhapsody of the Redwood

Tall redwoods sway in a wobbly dance,
While the shadows play, oh what a chance!
A woodpecker's beat, a rhythmic delight,
As laughter bursts forth in the moonlight.

The bumblebees buzz with a zany tune,
Spinning circles 'round the flowers in bloom.
A proud old owl gives a wise old wink,
As the creek gurgles, making us think.

The nature band gathers for a grand show,
With rabbits and badgers, friends in a row.
Each strum and hum sends a tickle around,
In this quirky orchestra of the ground.

As night draws near, the stars take stage,
Each twinkling light turns the page.
With giggles of grasshoppers, they all shout,
In this woodsy concert, there's never a doubt!

The Acorn Anthem

Acorns drop with a thump and a crash,
Making a tune, quite the comical splash.
The squirrels gather, it's time for a feast,
Planning mischief, they never missed.

Chirping birds provide a harmonious beat,
While shy little critters tap their feet.
A hedgehog rolls, causing laughter galore,
As they sing out loud, 'Can we have more?'

The wind joins in, a playful old friend,
Whispering secrets that never do end.
With rustling leaves and giggles around,
This acorn anthem is joyfully found.

So let the forest embrace all the cheer,
With woodland wonders, it's crystal clear.
In every note, every giggle and grin,
Nature's own laughter, where the fun begins!

Veneration in Verdant Rhythms

In a forest so grand, where the squirrels play,
The tree trunks dance lightly, day after day.
With roots that are ticklish, and branches that sway,
Even the sunbeams join in the ballet.

A fox with a hat, struts with such flair,
He tips it to owls, who all stop and stare.
With laughter and wiggles, they jiggle with glee,
The banter of branches, as funny as can be.

The pine trees gossip with ferns by their side,
Sharing tall tales of the things that they hide.
A worm in a top hat brings cake for a treat,
And everyone chuckles, oh what a fine feat!

The leaves start to giggle, the roots all conspire,
To throw the best party the woods can require.
As frogs sing the chorus of delight and cheer,
In this green little world, we forget all our fear.

Notes Amongst the Nectarines

In orchards of laughter, where fruits love to hum,
A peach plays the trumpet, quite silly and plumb.
The apples all gather, the bananas applaud,
Together they make this sweet garden a fraud.

The nectarines chuckle, with juice on their face,
The cherries start giggling, they think it's a race.
With toppings of laughter, they brighten the mood,
In this zesty fiesta, they're all in a good mood.

A bear wearing glasses recites all the rules,
While birds dive and soar, like a pack of old fools.
They prance with their sparrows in whimsical cheer,
In orchards of friendship, nothing's unclear.

As bees hum a tune, and the sun starts to fade,
The fruits share a secret, a jest that they made.
With laughter resounding, the day starts to close,
In this fruity kingdom, joy eternally flows.

A Chorus of the Wildflowers

In fields where the daisies wear crowns made of sun,
The wildflowers giggle, oh what jolly fun!
With petals that twirl and their stems all a-dance,
Each blossom insists on a chance for romance.

A ladybug winks at a tulip so bold,
While dandelions whisper sweet secrets untold.
The poppies all sway, draped in laughter and cheer,
Their colorful tunes echo far and near.

The sunflowers gossip with bees buzzing loud,
Claiming the title of 'Flower Queen' proud.
With pollen confetti fluttering around,
There's never a moment when laughter's not found.

As twilight arrives and the stars take their turn,
The wildflowers gather, their spirits still burn.
With roots that are tangled and dreams that take flight,
In fields of wild whimsy, they party all night.

The Glee of Growing Grasses

In meadows of giggles, where tall grasses sway,
They whisper and chuckle throughout the whole day.
With blades that are ticklish, they dance in the breeze,
As crickets join in with their own little tease.

A rabbit in slippers hops over with grace,
He slips on some dew, oh what a wild face!
The grasshoppers laugh, make a symphony bright,
In this leafy wonder, everything feels right.

With clovers for cushions, they lounge and eat snacks,
While fireflies twinkle, with shining green backs.
The daisies join in, holding hands above ground,
In this grassy gala, pure joy can be found.

As moonlight cascades on the giggly green crew,
A chorus of laughter bids nighttime adieu.
With shadows and whispers, the fun never ends,
In meadows of mirth, where the grass always bends.

The Forest's Lullaby

In the woods, where shadows play,
Squirrels dance and chirp away.
Leaves giggle in the sunny rays,
As trees sway in their leafy ballet.

Crickets sing a nightly tune,
Frogs croak back, a funny swoon.
Owls hoot jokes beneath the moon,
While fireflies flash, our nighttime boon.

Mice wear hats, they leap and bound,
In forest parties all around.
Beetles roll beneath the ground,
In this place, pure joy is found.

So lay your head on mossy bed,
Hear the laughs where nature's led.
With every creak and rustle said,
The forest giggles as you're fed.

Songs of the Cedar

Cedar branches sway on high,
Whispering secrets, oh my my!
The birds share tales in the sky,
While rabbits practice their lullaby.

Chipmunks wear their best attire,
Dancing round the campfire.
With acorns tossed, we conspire,
To poke fun without retire.

The sun sets low, the stars appear,
In this grove, we have no fear.
Nature's humor, loud and clear,
Comedic moments that endear.

Join the laughter, let it rise,
Beneath the moon with twinkling eyes.
In this forest, joy complies,
As cedar sings, we harmonize.

Harmony of the Pines

Pine trees stand as watchful guards,
In their shade, we let down our cards.
Squirrels share the latest bizarre,
While chipmunks juggle nuts and shards.

The breeze teases, tickles our cheeks,
As trees swap puns, oh what a week!
Beneath the roots, there hides a sneak,
A hedgehog snorts, a funny freak.

With every rustle, laughter grows,
The pines keep secrets, no one knows.
Through branches wide, the humor flows,
As evening falls, our joy bestows.

Under the stars, we'll sing aloud,
In this forest, we're all proud.
The harmony of laughter, vowed,
Together here, we form a crowd.

Chorus of the Cherries

In cherry trees, a feast we find,
With plump red fruits and jokes unlined.
The birds plot pranks, oh so refined,
As nature laughs, we unwind.

Worms wearing glasses, how absurd!
They read the news and share a word.
With every twist, the fun's assured,
In this orchard, joy's stirred.

As blossoms bloom, we share a cheer,
Gathering fruit and poking near.
The cherries giggle, casting jeer,
In this chorus, laughter's dear.

So pick a cherry, take a bite,
Nature's humor shines so bright.
In trees above, a playful sight,
We sing together, pure delight.

Rhythms of Rustling Leaves

Leaves danced and swayed,
In a breeze they played.
Squirrels slip and glide,
While acorns take a ride.

Branches start to jig,
A porcupine does a dig,
Frogs join in with croaks,
Making friends with the oaks.

The wind blows a tune,
As chipmunks start to croon.
Raccoons clap along,
In nature's merry throng.

With laughter in the air,
Nature's joy everywhere,
Each rustle is a beat,
Making music at our feet.

The Symphony of Stout Trees

Stout trees sway with pride,
In the forest, side by side.
Who needs a guitar?
When there's bark and bizarre.

Branches hum along,
Feeling nature's song.
Owls nod with delight,
As night falls, quite tight.

Bark scrapes together,
With laughter, light as feather.
Woodpeckers tap a rhyme,
In rhythm, they take time.

Underneath the moon,
We've found our silly tune.
For in every bough,
There's music here, right now.

Ballad of the Bark

Bark's a funny fellow,
Wrapped in colors, oh so yellow.
It giggles with the breeze,
Tickles leaves and makes them tease.

Squirrels whisper secrets,
In the shade where no one detects.
Bark rolls its eyes and grins,
While letting out some silly spins.

In the storm, it hums aloud,
Amongst the raucous, jolly crowd.
Together they shake and sway,
In a groovy, woodsy way.

Dance, oh bark, dance free,
In unity with every tree.
With each twist and turn, you spark,
The laughter of this happy park.

Chords from the Canopy

Canopy's vast dream,
Woven with sunlit beams.
Each branch strums a note,
While owls take to the coat.

The squirrels strum and pluck,
In their rhythm, there's no luck.
Pine cones drop like cymbals,
Adding to nature's symbols.

With every rustle, a laugh,
Nature's quirky autograph.
Leaves shimmy with delight,
In this joyous woodland night.

Harmony fills the air,
With nuts and jests to share.
Dancing in rustling glee,
In the canopy's melody.

Sonnet for the Swaying Branches

In the dance of leaves, they jive and spin,
Branches waving hello, just like good friends.
They tickle each other, with a gusty chuckle,
Swaying to the rhythm, beneath the skies' funnels.

A squirrel tries to salsa, with steady grace,
While birds cheer on, with a chirpy embrace.
The branches complain, 'Gosh, it's quite a riot!'
But together they sway, no tree wants to fight it.

Laughter in the woods, where squirrels take chance,
Bouncing in sync, they start a wild dance.
With twirls and with spins, oh what a delight,
Nature's own party, from morning till night.

So let us join in, and sway with the trees,
Giggling softly, dancing with ease.
In the embrace of branches, we find our play,
For fun in the forest is here to stay!

Overture of Overgrown Meadows

In meadows lush, the grass plays tricks,
With flowers marching in colorful kicks.
A bunny hops high, thinks he's got flair,
While dandelions giggle, toss hecklers in air.

The breeze carries tunes of insects so loud,
While tall blades of grass whisper, feeling quite proud.
A bumblebee buzzes, gets caught in a swirl,
As clovers all chuckle, watch their friend whirl.

Daisies do cartwheels, oh what a sight!
Painting the pastures with pure delight.
With shadows and sunlight, all mixing in glow,
They throw a grand fête, all put on a show!

Laughter erupts from creatures so small,
A symphony made, for the big and the tall.
Together they frolic, beneath the sky's blue,
In overgrown meadows, joy's always in view.

Rhapsody of Roots and Canopies

Beneath the big oak, the roots twist and pout,
Serving up rumors, both silly and stout.
They chatter and giggle, just out of earshot,
While the leaves overhead ponder, 'What have we got?'

The branches above, like a gossip brigade,
Spread tales of the winds that sweep through their shade.
With each rustling leaf, a new story is spun,
About the great storm, or the passing sun.

Squirrels twist round, with their tails in a twist,
A dance of confusion, squirrelly on the list.
Their chatter resounds, both clever and bright,
While the roots below snicker, 'What a fine sight!'

So here in the woods, both high and low,
The laughter of nature is all aglow.
With roots telling secrets and branches that play,
The world comes alive in a whimsical way!

The Song of Solitary Stumps

A stump stands alone, says, 'What a fine day!'
With grass growing wild, having its own play.
A frog jumps on top, with a croaky delight,
While daisies spin circles, in pure, silly flight.

Each ring tells a tale, of laughter and fights,
Of squirrels who zoomed, and birds who took flights.
'Oh, what a party' the mushrooms declare,
As they dance in a circle, without any care.

A gentle breeze whispers, 'Join in the fun!'
While shadows all stretch, as they bask in the sun.
The stump, once so quiet, now joins in the glee,
For laughter finds ways, where it wants to be free.

And though he's just wood, his heart's full of glee,
In this gathering spot, joy's boundless and free.
So together they chuckle, in the glow of the light,
The solitary stump, now gleaming so bright!

Cadence in the Clearing

In a forest so green and alive,
Squirrels dance, they twist and jive,
A woodpecker drums on a sturdy pine,
While rabbits hop, in a conga line.

Underneath branches, they play in glee,
A bear joins in with a clumsy spree,
Every creature lends a beat to the fun,
As sunlight dapples, they dance as one.

The leaves cheer on with a gentle rustle,
As frogs leap high, in a joyful hustle,
Nature's party, a rhythm divine,
Where every critter knows how to shine.

Laughter rings out, a bright melody,
In this clearing, wild and free,
With a swing of the tail and a twirl of a paw,
The forest laughs, it's a bouncy encore!

Notes from the Nook

In a cozy nook where laughter's loud,
A wise old owl surveys the crowd,
With his glasses perched on his beak,
He sings tales that make all creatures squeak.

Chirping crickets join in the tune,
With dancing fireflies under the moon,
A raccoon plays the pots and pans,
While the ants join in with their tiny hands.

Every whisper carries a quirky tale,
As badgers chuckle with their own style,
In every shadow, a giggle's found,
The nook hums softly, a joyful sound.

As night falls, the laughter will soar,
In this nook, there's always more,
With each little note, they fiddly-fought,
Creating a symphony that can't be bought.

Symphony of the Spruce

Beneath the spindly branches of a spruce,
A band of critters plays fast and loose,
With a hedgehog strumming a twig guitar,
And a moose tapping hooves, the star of the bar.

Squirrels leap with a nutty cheer,
While the raccoons pass around the beer,
In perfect harmony, they shake and spin,
As laughter echoes, it's a raucous din.

Then a skunk joins in with a pungent flair,
The crowd snickers, but they don't care,
They giggle and howl as the antics increase,
In this raucous symphony, fun won't cease.

As the sun dips low, they take their bows,
For this wild concert—the forest allows,
With every brush of the softest breeze,
Nature claps, and they dance with ease.

Refrain of the Roots

Deep in the earth where the funny things brew,
The roots all chuckle, as rumors ensue,
A gopher spreads tales of a mishap so grand,
While a wise old toad gives a flip of his hand.

With each little jig of a mossy toe,
The laughter erupts like a bubbly show,
A chorus of giggles, so sweet and spry,
The roots hum a tune that'll never die.

In this underground, joyous parade,
Every plant and critter plays masquerade,
Rabbits and moles join the light-hearted jest,
With grins on their faces, they're feeling blessed.

As night whispers softly to the vibrant ground,
The refrain of the roots is a giggly sound,
So come one, come all, to this earthy delight,
Where the roots make music from morning till night!

Melodies of the Moonlit Grove

In the grove where shadows play,
Bouncing bunnies join the fray.
Trees are dancing, swaying light,
Singing songs throughout the night.

Owls are hooting silly tunes,
Tickling leaves like happy loons.
Raccoons arrive with a band,
Drumming paws on soft, cool sand.

Songs in the Silvan Shadows

When the moon begins to grin,
Squirrels gather, let's begin!
Acorns bouncing, laughter spreads,
Underneath their leafy beds.

Caterpillars slide and glide,
Joining in the nighttime ride.
They wiggle-waggle, twirling round,
Crickets chirp a funny sound.

Celestial Cadence of Pine

Pine trees whisper, soft and sweet,
While the chipmunks tap their feet.
Harmonies of barking dogs,
Mix with croaking from the frogs.

Breezes giggle through the leaves,
Making music, who believes?
Frogs in ties hold a debate,
On who sings the best first-rate!

Lullabies of the Leafy Realm

Underneath the starlit sky,
Wander bugs that flutter by.
Glowworms shine with little winks,
While the willow softly blinks.

Fireflies start a lively dance,
Making everyone take a chance.
Jumping joyfully in a line,
Nature's party, oh so fine!

Echoing Through the Evergreens

In the forest, a squirrel sings,
With acorns bouncing, oh, the flings!
The wise old owl gives a hoot,
While rabbits dance in furry boots.

Trees sway gently, clapping hands,
While deer in circles make their stands.
A breeze whispers, 'Let's go play!'
As branches join in on the fray.

A chipmunk joins with quite a flair,
In a hat and coat, oh, what a pair!
Echoes of laughter fill the air,
Nature's jesters, beyond compare.

Nature's Musical Motif

The brook hums softly, a bubbly tune,
While frogs croak out, a merry croon.
Birds chirp wildly in chorus bright,
Creating symphonies, pure delight.

A caterpillar plays the flute,
Underneath the leafy suit.
Woodpeckers drum on trees so high,
Their rhythm makes the branches sigh.

With critters lining up to dance,
The forest floor will take its chance.
Sap oozing down in sticky globs,
To every beat, the nature mobs.

Aria of the Autumnal Forest

Leaves are laughing, twirling down,
In vibrant hues, they wear a crown.
A voice of wind, a rustling twist,
In this grand show, none can resist.

Squirrels boast of winter hoards,
In chirps and giggles, all in cords.
Bears stomp by in rhythm slow,
While hedgehogs quietly steal the show.

Fungi rise up, as the stage crew,
With pop-up hats, what a view!
Each creature plays a quirky part,
In this whimsical, nature's art.

Cadence of the Conifers

Pine needles rustle, a quirky beat,
While critters hop on little feet.
The wind shakes branches, a gentle strum,
As laughter echoes, it can't be glum.

With squirrel duets and raccoon cheers,
Forest friends conquer all their fears.
A chorus of buzzes fills the air,
As bumbles dance without a care.

Mice with flutes and raccoons with drums,
Join in the fun as everyone hums.
In shades of green, they twirl and play,
Nature's extravaganza, every day.

Verses from the Verdant Depths

In a forest of green, a squirrel did dance,
Chasing his tail with a curious prance.
The trees all giggled, they swayed in delight,
As he spun in circles, a comical sight.

A bear in a bowtie, so dapper and neat,
Tried to sip honey, but fell on his feet.
The bees all buzzed, they chuckled with glee,
At the sight of the bear, sticky and free.

Rabbits played banjos, while owls sang along,
In a jam by the stream, they strummed out a song.
The frogs joined the chorus with croaks loud and clear,
While the ducks quacked in time, bringing cheers.

A moose wearing glasses read comic books bright,
He stumbled on roots, oh what a silly sight!
The trees kept on laughing, the wind blew so strong,
In the depths of the forest, life danced along.

The Whirlwind's Wooded Waltz

A whirlwind blew through, with a whoosh and a swirl,
As the leaves took to dancing, a flurry, a twirl.
A frog in a top hat said, 'Let's throw a ball!'
He tripped on a twig and he fell with a sprawl.

Foxes in tuxedos played pranks on the frogs,
While the owls looked on, puffing up like old logs.
With each little hop and each fluttering wing,
The forest erupted, oh, what joy they'd bring!

A raccoon with rhythm played drums made of bark,
While crickets sang tunes till the sun slipped to dark.
The rabbits all cheered, on their little feet bound,
For the waltz of the woods had the wildest sound.

In the night, as they twirled beneath the moon's glow,
The laughs echoed softly in the heart of the grove.
Amidst all the antics, the fun never ceased,
In the whirlwind's waltz, there was joy released.

Whispers of the Woodlands

In a glade filled with giggles, the critters conspire,
A chipmunk, a jester, with jokes to admire.
He told a tall tale about a snail on a quest,
Who raced with a turtle, but took a long rest.

The badger, so wise, gave advice with a grin,
'Always carry a snack for the long journeys in!'
As they chuckled together, the trees smiled wide,
For the joy of the woods was their favorite guide.

The squirrels threw acorns like balls made of gold,
But one hit a rabbit, who squeaked, 'Oh, so bold!'
They laughed till they cried, 'What a ridiculous throw!'
In the whispers of woodlands, the humor did flow.

A woodpecker drummed out a fast-paced beat,
While raccoons broke into a dance with swift feet.
The night wrapped them snug in a blanket of fun,
In the woodlands' soft whispers, all worries were done.

Echoes in the Canopy

In the canopy high, where the sunlight peeks,
A parrot told stories in colorful squeaks.
His tales were a mix of the foolish and grand,
Of a hippo who fancied a pint of fine sand.

A squirrel, quite nutty, threw acorns for sport,
He miscalculated, and hit a bear's snort.
With a growl and a shake, he looked quite dismayed,
While the forest erupted in laughter displayed.

The owls in their wisdom hooted out loud,
As the woodpeckers danced, each feeling quite proud.
With each little flap, and each caw in the air,
The echoes of mischief filled spirits with flair.

As night cloaked the forest in shadows and light,
The giggles and guffaws brought warmth through the night.
In the echoes of trees, tales of humor were spun,
In the heart of the woods, every creature had fun.

www.ingramcontent.com/pod-product-compliance
Lightning Source LLC
Chambersburg PA
CBHW071812160426
43209CB00003B/60